HOW JEZEBEL HIJACKS PROPHETIC MINISTRY

by Jonas Clark

Unless otherwise noted, Scripture quotations are taken from the King James Version.

HOW JEZEBEL HIJACKS PROPHETIC MINISTRY
ISBN-10: 1-886885-46-X
ISBN-13: 978-1-886885-46-2

Published by Jonas Clark Ministries
27 West Hallandale Beach Blvd.
Hallandale, Florida, 33009-5437, U.S.A.
(954) 456-4420

www.JonasClark.com

HOW JEZEBEL HIJACKS PROPHETIC MINISTRY

The phone rang today. A teary-eyed young woman, we'll call her Sally, on the other end called one of our prayer counselors at the ministry saying,

> "I- I want to thank Jonas for writing about the spirit of Jezebel."

Our ministry often receives calls from readers facing something they don't quite know how to handle. This call, however, was even more sobering. She told the story of living in a small rural town in heartland America. She said her husband and children love God with all their hearts and are faithful attendees to their church. She continued,

> "At our church there is a woman who wanted to recruit me. I didn't get a witness and needed to pray about it a bit more. After several weeks of hounding me she began to prophesy that God was calling me to work with her. Again, I didn't have an inner witness to that prophetic word of prophecy. When I didn't receive the prophetic word, she told me I was in rebellion against God and my children would come under a curse.

Later that night I told my husband what she prophesied. Being just simple believers we decided that we should talk with the pastor about it. We love our church and it's one of the fastest growing in our area. People come from miles around to attend. We love God too and are just regular people. We don't have any ministerial training and just want to serve Jesus the best way we know how. We were brought up in a denominational church and don't have much experience in a Spirit-filled church with 'prophetic people.' I'm so disturbed over this." As she paused to wipe away more tears. "Our pastor accepted an appointment from me. When I told him what the woman prophesied over me that I should work with her and when I refused she told me that God said that rebellion

I would encourage all my brothers and sisters in Christ to resist unscriptural malice and control even when delivered with a spiritual sounding "thus sayeth the Lord."

endangered my children's lives, to my utter surprise, the pastor closed his office door, lowered his voice, also prophesied over me saying that the Holy Spirit told him that I should work with the woman and stop being such a &*^%$&* (explicative not included)."

Friend, this dear woman was heart broken. Through sobs she told the rest of her testimony of prophetic error at her church. I would be shocked with her call except we have fielded related calls before. Many questions arise when we hear things like this such as: "What's happening to the prophetic ministry within our Spirit-filled and Charismatic churches across our nation?" Is it possible the prophetic ministry is being hijacked by another spirit? Has the Jezebel spirit so seduced and deceived that we fail to see the control, manipulation and absolute putrescence within certain circles? Why has prophetic ministry become so mystical, ambiguous, equivocal and superspiritual? Why do some freely curse our nation, leaders, the children of God and others in the name of the Lord when scripture specifically says, "bless and curse not?" (Romans 12:14).

Is it possible we need correction, even reformation within the Church regarding prophetic ministry? Where are the protectors of the Cross? Who's responsible for the well-being of the children of God? What is the purpose of prophecy anyway? Is it to judge and condemn, scold and wangle? Is it a mean-spirited operation? (1 Corinthians 13:2). What is the fruit of prophetic ministry in America? Are thousands repenting of their sins and coming to Christ? Are the hearts of the fathers turning toward the sons and the sons toward the fathers?

Should we dare ask any questions?

Is there any mercy, grace, faith, hope or peace offered toward the people of God and our country? Is personal prophesy manifesting Christ, the spirit of prophesy? Is it true that this woman's children would fall under a curse for not obeying this woman's prophetic utterance? Did this pastor step out of line and sully the spirit of prophesy? Is his apparent success in ministry validated because the church is large and growing? What should our response be? Are we experiencing true prophetic ministry when such utterances are spoken in the name of the Lord? That's many questions I know.

I am convinced that all personal prophesy should be judged according to Scripture that is given

> "by inspiration of God and is profitable for doctrine, for reproof, for correction, for instruction in righteousness that the man of God may be perfect, thoroughly furnished unto all good works" (2 Timothy 3:16-17).

The Word says,

> "Believe not every spirit, but try the spirits whether they are of God..." (1 John 4:1).

Jezebel is a prophetic spirit and demonic warrior. She can be bold, crafty, subtle, aloof and daring. She can teach, preach and prophesy better than any one you have ever met.

That means put what is said to you on trial, and don't be afraid to do it. I would encourage all my brothers and sisters in Christ to resist unscriptural malice and control even when delivered with a spiritual sounding "thus sayeth the Lord." And it doesn't matter how well known the person is or how many television shows he or she has appeared on, all prophecy should be examined.

I would like to appeal to you old-timers in the Lord, guardians and friends of the faith that were raised around the Holy Ghost to help those in this generation rightly divide the Word of Truth and to understand the sensible, loving and gentle ways of the Holy Spirit and to look to God, not man, even prophetic ones, for counsel, wisdom and direction. Derek Prince once said regarding the manifestation of the Spirit, "The manifestation of the Spirit is always given for a useful, practical, sensible purpose."

So what would your counsel be to a heartbroken family that feels so sad? Some might say this family needs to stay in the church and work it out. Often I would agree. This, however, is startling and distressing. Does one really need a faux prophetic word as a recruiting tool? Yes, Christ's Church is a respected place that I love dearly but if Jezebel is free to operate with the approval of leadership in any particular community then that husband has a responsibility, even a duty as the priest of his house, to take his wife and family out of harms way without delay as they search for another fellowship.

"But what of prophetic words and the spirit of prophecy," you ask? Scripture declares, "Despise not prophesyings" (1 Thessalonians 5:20). We do, however, have a responsibility to,

> "Study to show yourself approved unto God, a workman that needeth not to be ashamed, rightly dividing the word of truth. But shun profane and vain babblings: (especially prophetic ones) for they will increase unto more ungodliness" (2 Timothy 2:15-16).

Jezebel is a prophetic spirit and demonic warrior. She can be bold, crafty, subtle, aloof and daring. She

The Spirit of God inside of you is opposing the spiritual climate around you. The reason you feel uncomfortable in your spirit sometimes is because your spirit will contend with things unseen.

---

can teach, preach and prophesy better than any one you have ever met. She's public at times and concealed at others. She waits, she stalks, she seizes in moments of weakness, your weakness. She is, in her own stead, a giant killer, God's giants. Many have fallen by her sword. Her life is full of chaos, confusion, sexual sin, perversions many, and fear. She knows the Word of God but refuses to live by it.

In my book I called her *"Jezebel, Seducing Goddess of War"* and that's exactly what this spirit is as she declares herself the unseen "lady of kingdoms" (Isaiah 47).

CONFRONTATION WITH JEZEBEL

I met the Jezebel spirit early on in my prophetic ministry and quickly became intimately acquainted with her wicked ways. Shortly after this brief introduction I found myself being resisted on all fronts, yet I didn't completely understand what that resistance was. You see, Jezebel was yet an unnamed foe. The Jezebel spirit was at that time a mysterious rival that seemed to know me quite well. It was as if she had studied my strengths and weaknesses as she prepared to wage an all-out war against me.

While I had a revelation of spiritual warfare and binding and loosing, this spiritual war was somehow different and the victory was not swift. The root of the resistance was deeply planted in the spiritual realm. Whoever this unseen rival was, it was not giving up easily. It wasn't even backing down.

I still remember pacing around my backyard in prayer and intercession for hours at a time during those days. What felt like an intense grieving would come upon me regularly and all I could do was cry out to God to unlock the mystery. The grieving intensified and I realized I was in a spiritual war far greater than anything I had experienced in the past. It was a spiritual clash against an unidentified enemy. I can't do justice to the feelings with mere words. Suffice it to say that I knew I was under a vicious spiritual attack. And vicious is still too mild a word. I knew I was in a spiritual war against an especially wicked foe.

It is critical to understand who your enemy is, and for our own protection God will not send us into battle without preparing us.

This went on for months until one day I heard a minister explaining an experience that was markedly similar to mine. He described the emotions of his soul and even the physical symptoms associated with contending with a spirit called "Jezebel" and he explained that he had to learn how to fight the Jezebel spirit so he could launch his ministry.

When I heard him say that, something went off inside of me (an inner witness) and I thought, "That's the same thing that I feel, in my spirit, when I walk around my backyard praying." Once I knew what I was fighting against, I began to study the Word of God for revelation on the wicked wiles of this Jezebel spirit.

Perhaps you are feeling the same spiritual clash. When you feel that clash it could be because the Jezebel spirit is targeting and attacking you or because the Spirit of God inside of you is opposing the spiritual climate around you. The reason you feel uncomfortable in your spirit sometimes is because your spirit will contend with things unseen. Scripture declares,

> "For we wrestle not against flesh and blood, but against principalities, against powers, against the rulers of the darkness of this world, against spiritual wickedness in high places" (Ephesians 6:12).

When God was training me for the ministry He taught me about these things in my backyard so that I would not be ignorant of the devil's devices when He sent me to the nations (2 Corinthians 2:11). It is critical to understand who your enemy is, and for our own protection God will not send us into battle without preparing us. The Holy Spirit Himself taught me how to fight against and conquer the Jezebel spirit through prayer and intercession. And once I conquered her, the Lord put it on my heart to write a book to help others break free from Jezebel, the seducing goddess of war.

Are you contending with this unseen Jezebel spirit that is trying to destroy your life, family, ministry and future? Brothers and sisters, you must be well prepared to contend with the Jezebel spirit, God desires to equip all of His children to live a victorious Christian life here and now.

Read one reader's testimony of a young preacher's kid from Michigan who discovered the Jezebel spirit operating in his parents' church. What was worse, this Jezebel spirit was on the praise and worship team and attempted to wreak havoc in the sanctuary every chance she got. Listen to Billy's testimony...

JEZEBEL'S ATTEMPT TO HINDER THE HOLY SPIRIT

"I am a 21-year-old minister at my parents' church. My mom and dad are called as a prophetess and apostle. I am called as a prophet myself. I wanted to share with you some of the things I have seen Jezebel do in our church.

At first we did not know it was Jezebel, but as we learned more about her traits we

She's public at times and concealed at others. She waits, she stalks, she seizes in moments of weakness, your weakness. She is, in her own stead, a giant killer, God's giants.

---

soon realized whom we were dealing with. This spirit moved through people at our church. One in particular was our praise and worship leader. At times when she would lead worship I would hear something screech almost like a bird. At first I thought it was the sound equipment acting up, but it would be so painful I couldn't stand it. She was purposely messing up. When the Holy Spirit would finally fall she would cut us off and butcher the song. She couldn't stand the prophetic voice even when coming through songs. That spirit was seducing and flattering one minute and would cut you the next.

I have seen men on fire for God and when they married a Jezebel they would be emasculated. They would look old and drained as if they had no life. Just recently the Lord told me to name the youth department "Jehu Generation." He said He was going to raise up warriors with a word in their mouth and a sword in their hand that would destroy Jezebel and Baal and not compromise. I had my doubts about the name because I thought it was extreme, but I know that the Lord told me this. Now I see why I am going through attacks. Jezebel doesn't want me to walk in my destiny."

Like Billy I pray that you will learn to resist and overcome the Jezebel spirit in your ministries and churches for the sake of your families and nations.

Christ had something to say to the leaders of His governing churches that ignored the Jezebel spirit.

"Notwithstanding I have a few things against thee, because thou sufferest (you know she is in your ministry and don't do anything to stop her) that woman Jezebel, which calleth herself a prophetess (a prophetic spirit), to teach and to seduce my servants....And I gave her space to repent of her fornication and she repented not. Behold, I will cast her into a bed, and them that commit adultery with her into great tribulation (stress beyond belief), except they repent of their deeds. And I will kill her children with death and all the churches shall know that I am he which searcheth the reins and hearts (the motives of people including their prophetic words): and I will give unto every one of you according to your works" (Revelation 2:20-23).

I am reminded of Christ' prophetic word that every demonic spirit, especially the spirit of Jezebel, needs to hear, "I will build my church and the gates of hell will not prevail against it."

ISBN 1-886885-32-X

HOW WITCHCRAFT SPIRITS ATTACK

There are spiritual forces of witchcraft working to destroy your life, ministry and future. Scripture teaches that you are in a spiritual war.

Discover your authority:

- How to recognize an attack.
- How to stop the powers of control.
- How to overcome weariness and fatigue.
- How to break demonic soul ties.
- What to do when attacked by confusion.
- And much more...

Order How Witchcraft Spirits Attack online at www.JonasClark.com or call 800.943.6490.

ISBN 1-886885-25-7

EFFECTIVE MINISTRIES & BELIEVERS:
INTRODUCING APOSTOLIC MINISTRY AND WHAT IT MEANS TO YOU

Christ's disciples have fought raging spiritual battles with Satan for centuries. Some failed, others experienced limited success, but there is another group, effective believers that discovered the secret to victorious living. This group was taught by apostles that Christ would "build His Church and the gates of hell would not prevail against it."

Those who want to do great exploits for Christ need to read this book.

Discover your authority:
- How the apostles taught believers to turn the world upside down.
- How apostolic design empowers every believer for breakthrough.
- How to become a spiritual warrior, reformer and prophetic strategists.
- How apostolic restoration and reformation principles advance your calling.

Order Effective Ministries and Believers online at www.JonasClark.com or call 800.943.6490.

PROPHECY WITHOUT PERMISSION

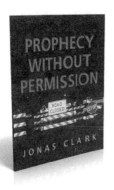

ISBN 1-886885-31-1

Presumptous prophets prophesy because they can, but should they? Does a prophet need permission to prophesy? If a prophet who has not been granted permission to prophesy and yet does, is he guilty of sin.

**Prophetic ministry is important and so is accuracy.
Learn these truths:**

- How prophets stay accurate.
- Why prophecy by faith alone is dangerous.
- How to avoid the spirit of divination.
- Five steps to prophetic release.
- Prophetic Mantels and Activation.
- Receiving prophetic permission.

MORE EASY READ POCKET-SIZE BOOKS BY JONAS CLARK

Pocket-Size Books

Entering Prophetic Ministry
Prophecy Without Permission
How Witchcraft Spirits Attack
Seeing What Others Can't
Unlocking Prophetic Imaginations
What To Do When You Feel Like Giving Up
The Weapons Of Your Warfare
Overcoming Dark Imaginations
Healing Rejection and Emotional Abuse
Breaking Christian Witchcraft
Prophetic Confrontations
Unlocking Spiritual Authority
Avoiding Foreign Spirits
How Jezebel Hijacks Prophetic Ministry
How Prophets Fail
Identifying Prophetic Spiritists

www.JonasClark.com

Equipping Resources by Jonas Clark

Books

Extreme Prophetic Studies

Advanced Apostolic Studies

Kingdom Living: How to Activate Your Spiritual Authority

Imaginations: Dare to Win the Battle Against Your Mind

Jezebel, Seducing Goddess of War *(Also Available in Spanish)*

Exposing Spiritual Witchraft

30 Pieces of Silver *(Overcoming Religious Spirits)*

The Apostolic Equipping Dimension

Effective Ministries & Believers

Life After Rejection: God's Path to Emotional Healing

Come Out! A Handbook for the Serious Deliverance Minister

Saboteurs in The Republic: Battling Spiritual Wickedness in High Places

www.JonasClark.com